After All That We've Been Through

Verse for What's Truly Important in Life

By R. Olin Jackson

Published by Whippoorwill Publications, LLC
Roswell, Georgia

Copyright 2024 by R. Olin Jackson III
All Rights Reserved, including the right to reproduce this book
in portions thereof or in any form whatsoever
whether by traditional or electronic means,
except for brief quotations used in promotion of this book.

ISBNs: 979-8-9900211-0-5 (b&w trade edition);
979-8-9900211-1-2 (color premium edition)

Library of Congress Control Number: 2024902403

Publisher's Cataloging-in-Publication Data
provided by Five Rainbows Cataloging Services
Names: Jackson III, Ralph Olin, 1951- author.
Title: After all that we've been through : verse for what's truly
   important in life / R. Olin Jackson.
Description: Roswell, GA : Whippoorwill Publications, 2024. |
   Includes index.
Identifiers: LCCN 2024902403 (print) | ISBN 979-8-9900-211-0-5
   (hardcover : b&w) | ISBN 979-8-9900211-1-2 (hardcover : color)
Subjects: LCSH: Georgia—Poetry. | Spiritual life—Poetry. | Life—
   Poetry. | Autobiographical poetry. | Autobiographical poetry,
   American. | BISAC: POETRY / American / General. | POETRY /
   Subjects & Themes / Inspirational & Religious. | BIOGRAPHY &
   AUTOBIOGRAPHY / General.
Classification: LCC PS3610.A25 A38 2024 (print) | LCC PS3610.
   A25 (ebook) | DDC 811/.6—dc23.

*Lovingly Dedicated To:
Judy Kay Grizzle Jackson*

Author of:

Moonshine, Murder & Mayhem in Georgia (2003)
Georgia Backroads Traveler (2005)
Mystery & History in Georgia, Volume 1 (2022)
Mystery & History in Georgia, Volume 2 (2023)
Some Genealogy Keys to Some Georgia Family Trees (2023)
Memories of Army Life and MPs of the 529th (2023)
John Henry "Doc" Holliday (2023)
Gunmen, Lawmen & Wild Men of Early Georgia (2024)

Cover painting of Christmas scene by Tatiana Mack, "YaneyaArt," Alpharetta, Georgia.

Copies of Whippoorwill Publications, LLC books are available online at Amazon.com; BarnesandNoble.com; IngramSpark.com; and other fine booksellers.

Contents

Foreword vii

It's God That Made It So 3
Are We Really All Equal in Heaven? 5
Life Slips Away 7
A Love Letter To Judy 9
The Children of Springtime 11
Time's A Harsh Mistress 13
Falling Leaves 16
We Are But Keepers 18
A Song for Mary 20
The Birthday Cake 23
A "Little Big" Mistake 24
The Barefoot Boy 26
About the Author 37
Photos Index 39

Foreword

As a child on a cold Christmas Eve in a country farmhouse in the early 1950s, R. Olin Jackson sat mesmerized before a crackling warm fire in the hearth at his family home in the mountains of northwest Georgia, as his father read – in a deep sonorous voice – Clement Clarke Moore's immortal *"T'was The Night Before Christmas."* Olin, his brother, David, and sisters Patricia and Mary were fascinated and awed by this wonderfully-lyrical work of art, just as children occasionally continue to be even today. The unique verse in Moore's poem introduced Olin to the inspirational world of that art and its poignant influences upon life.

Even though he didn't know it at the time, poetry was to become incremental to Olin's life. Inspired by such masterpieces as Robert Frost's *"Stopping By Woods on a Snowy Evening,"* the captivating Kipling's *"If,"* John Greenleaf Whittier's *"The Barefoot Boy,"* and the incomparable Longfellow's *"The Wreck of the Hesperus,"* Olin eventually began making lyrical attempts of his own.

On the pages which follow, a handful of those efforts are presented for the reader. In these heart-felt simple works, Olin has presented a picture of, perhaps, the forces at work as one pursues his or her daily life, and further, musings of the manner in which the Almighty demonstrates to each and every one of us what truly is important in this life so fleeting. . . .

*"After all that we've been through,
I find that when I think of you,
A warm south wind blows through and through,
And in my heart there's only you."*

Gregory LeNoir Allman
Excerpt from "The Queen of Hearts" (1973)

After All That We've Been Through

It's God That Made It So

By R. Olin Jackson

All creatures on the earth snow-white;
How do they really know,
that 'neath the white, in its frostbite
their food lies in the snow?

How do the birds on Heaven's wing
know where to find their feed?
They search beneath the leaves and things
and there discover seed.

The fox can smell the mouse hid well.
The mole does burrow deep,
to eat the roots and tender shoots
before its long slow sleep.

How does the deer upon the slopes
find sustenance so rare?
How does it know to nip the bud?
Why does it even care?

How do the bugs and slimy slugs
survive the cold onslaught?
From where do they, arrive the day
that spring again is brought?

Through life's travails, its peaks and vales,
our lives can seem so bleak.
So few do pause in wondrous awe
of all we take so cheap.

For all we gather from the sow
and chance to pack and keep,
most often does the credit go,
to someone else but He.

So now you know that in the snow
the animals do find
their food, their home, their will to grow,
from Someone wise and kind.

So who created "Nature's" Theme?
How do the creatures know?
That's easy friend; so simple for
it's God that made it so.

Are We Really All Equal in Heaven?

By R. Olin Jackson

Are there past sinners in Heaven
who frequent the Lord's "lesser seats,"
whose deeds have caused them to waiver
their chances for higher Retreat?

Some no doubt gain their admission
despite lives of much villainy
by trusting the Lord as a Christian,
in last-minute expiring pleas.

Those who did dally on Sunday
too lazy for church to attend.
Those who so often dictated,
to others the wages of sin.

Those who chose crime their profession
assaulting the innocent meek.
Those with evil obsessions
preying on others too weak.

How can such souls receive solace
in Heaven with all of its saints?
How can their earthly-spent horrors
avoid earning Satan's restraints?

Tis hard to imagine "bad sinners"
existing in equal sublime;
along with those barely committing
far less Biblical crimes.

Knowing we only reach Heaven
believing He rose from the Grave;
Are we There equally ever,
with many who "barely" were Saved?

Despite all this we have to trust Him;
have faith in His Holy Design.
For in the end it hardly matters,
when we our last breath do resign.

Life Slips Away

By R. Olin Jackson

Spring-times of life seem so endless;
when one is a child with no woes;
but years slip away far too quickly,
as children grow up and grow old.

Silently streaming; steadily trickling;
years show no thought of retreat.
Life gives not even an inkling
of what one will finally meet.

To youngsters alike the world over,
life's ending is hardly a thought.
They rise each day in rapt composure,
to see what the new day has brought.

So much in life we take for granted,
With far too much wasted in woe.
A pity we're not more committed,
to serving those needy and low.

Our life is an uncharted issue,
filled with mistakes and gross waste.
We rarely note our true mission,
while selfishly acting in haste.

Why does one so seldom notice
that life is much more than just "me?"
Why do we ne'er stop to focus,
on helping poor souls in life's sea?

When all of the years are depleted
and bodies are poor weakened sights,
lost souls still remain so conceited
they cannot admit their sad plight.

As one looks back on those wages;
It finally dawns on lost souls.
There now is a price for the ages,
as written in God's Sacred Scrolls.
.

A Love Letter To Judy

By R. Olin Jackson

Here we are. . . 4-0 and counting;
all the years so swiftly mounting.
Who would have thought?
Who could have known?
I'd be the lucky one to own. . .

A love so strong and so complete. . . .
I'm filled with awe at what we keep.
With the breath I take each day,
I thank dear God for love so sweet.
I thank dear God we chanced to meet.

Has it been smooth? . . . . Has it been charmed?
Quite frankly "No," but what's the harm?
What 'ere the price our love must cost,
is minor to what would be lost,
is worth the frenzied sea we're tossed.

Your love the strength of life to me,
As bright your smile I daily see.
A love you have steadfastly given,
all to me and quite unbidden;
like an Angel down from Heaven.

Now I often pause to ponder;
How I once did seek to wander.
There simply is no way today;
no way that I could live without,
Your love so sweet and so devout.

Now we're old with hair of grey.
Old age I wish was far away.
Yet each night when I do sleep,
each night in slumber oh so deep,
your love a treasure I do keep.
Your love a treasure oh so sweet.

The Children of Springtime

By R. Olin Jackson

Night by night, day by day -
where did the hours go?
We worked at play and played at work
as time moved oh so slow.

Tis like a dream remembered,
in golden-hued sunsets.
When life was still a wonder
for those with no regrets.

Memories from springtime.
Strawberries from the field.
Laughter in our running -
no worries yet revealed.

The boys a fort on hillsides.
The girls with dolls to hold.
Mom and Dad together.
Ne'er a want nor woe.

Mom's warm arms in mornings.
All our needs are met.
New sun the sky a'borning.
Not a thing to dread.

As long as Dad would hold us
and read verse from his past,
our eyes all held such wonder,
though tears from Dad's streamed fast.

For life does so deceive us,
through all its ebbs and flows,
to think it ne'er will leave us
regardless of the blows.

High school then college swiftly
reach us far too soon.
Quick as winds a'whistling,
the youth fades from our bloom.

The nest now long abandoned
with young ones grown and tall.
But Mom and Dad yet homeward,
unerring toward the "Fall."

Time's A Harsh Mistress

By R. Olin Jackson

The march of Time once friend of mine;
it seemed to last so long.
Back in the days of life sublime,
when I was young and strong.

Time seemed to me an endless game,
a thing of long duress.
But in the end a tragic shame,
cause Time's a harsh mistress.

The days slip by in idle song;
a chasing of the wind.
When I was young and life was long
Time seemed like such a friend.

I wish I'd known the fate I'd face
when Time was closing in.
I wish I'd known I had no ace
cause Time was not my friend.

When swept along within the throng
we just don't comprehend,
that soon we'll sing a different song,
as Time draws to the end.

When comes that day you're not so young,
when breath you can't take in,
you'll wish a different route you'd run,
in days of youth and sin.

So heed my words; don't waste your time.
Of this I strongly stress.
Cause in the end you'll also find
that Time's a harsh mistress.

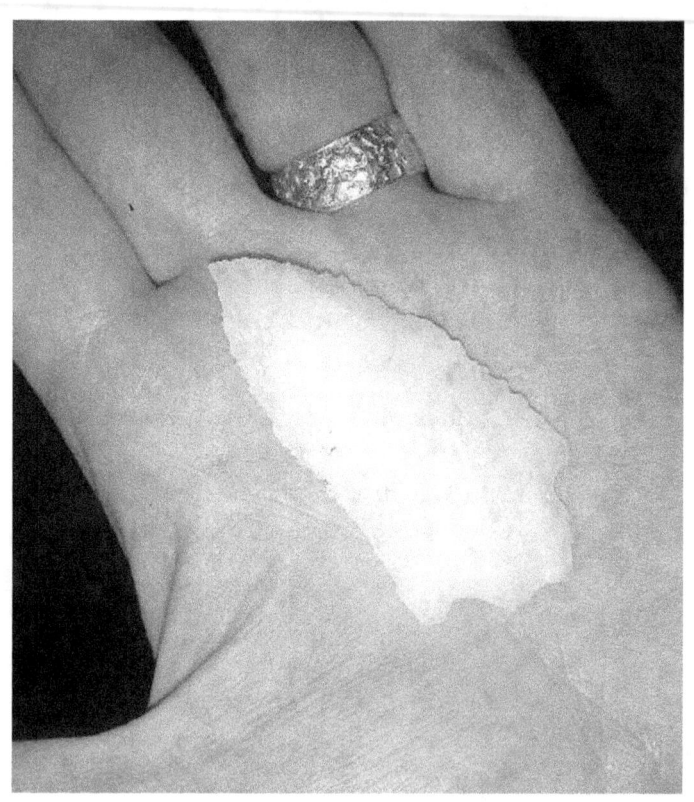

Falling Leaves

By Essie Hudgins Jordan & R. Olin Jackson

Tumbling, gliding, floating down,
soon to settle on the ground.
Nature's carpet on the grass
we may marvel as we pass.

They seem to gasp *"Walk softly please*
"for we are all still lovely leaves.
"Though brown and now into decay,
"we still protect on cold dark days."

God from Whom all blessings flow
supplies these leaves to us to show
that in the spring we grow til fall,
but in the fall we wither all.

On faded stem all leaves do toil,
until they float down to the soil,
providing nutrients for trees
which in turn produce new leaves.

God's miracle repeats each year
a tiny part of His great Sphere.
We all should therefore humbly note
we all will likewise one day float.

We Are But Keepers

By R. Olin Jackson

We are but keepers all
slow-moving thru this life,
collecting prints, new toys and scrawl,
and saving for twilight.

Each day we pass in this morass
planning how we might,
collect still more of this repast,
to lock up snug and tight.

We keep our jewels shiny bright;
We love the Chevy's roar.
Each closet's full of fashion's sights
to which our lust cries "More!"

We keep the house, a boat, a bar;
we think our life is long.
But He'll remind you from afar
that tact's just all dead wrong.

Still we save, we steal, we stall,
just to pack it back.
And yet the birds on wing each fall,
have logic we all lack.

For all the "things" the "toys" and "stuff"
to which we're so inclined,
have zero value in the end.
It's all just left behind.

So when you wrap your life around
possessions all piled high,
I hope I won't be thought unsound,
when adding with a sigh:

"When we're at the end of life
our 'stuff' we are forbidden.
"The only thing we 'keep' in Flight
is the love we've given."

A Song for Mary

By R. Olin Jackson

Baby girl dresses.
Long golden tresses.
Sometimes in dreams
she's still here it seems.

Tight-woven pigtails.
Quick feet down the trail.
Carefree to a fault.
Sweet sis worries naught.

Dad and Mom here;
there's nothing to fear.
Whispers of chatter;
Soft barefoot patter.

In visions and dreams,
all sweetness it seems,
I see her in mornings;
old school days aborning.

A nickname of "Missy,"
so dainty and prissy.
A squall and a splatter;
"Oh! What's the matter?"

Soft words to her lips.
Mispronounced slips.
"Hang-coater," "mow-lawner."
Sweet whisperings from her.

Through all she'd just smile,
a face naught with guile.
Through all that she passed,
Miss Mary had class.

Possessed of true courage,
she never worried.
Double-quick wit.
At the devil she'd spit.

Pain though at home
so she had to roam.
Said that the highway
would be her new byway.

Fashionable dresses;
still golden tresses.
Soon she's all grown;
tall, tanned, hair wind-blown.

A soft-spoken sigh;
twinkle in her eye,
sparkling with grace
in womanly lace.

Through good times and bad,
some really sad,
she always had style.
She never knew trial.

Though smiles lit her face,
her life held no ace.
So sad in the end,
no way she might mend.

Courageous and tall
she faced every fall.
Magnificent might,
waged in her fight.

You're never alone
sweet sister our own.
Reach up touch His Face.
You're in His Embrace.

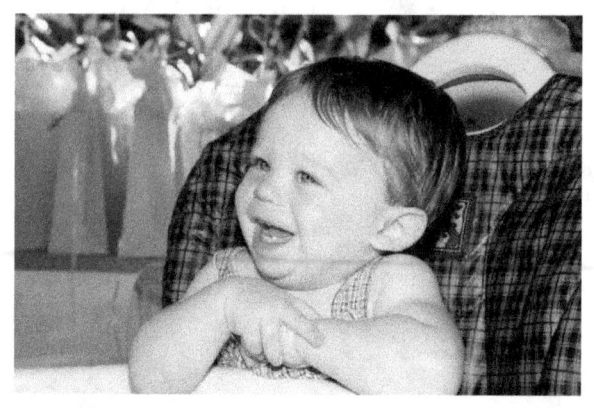

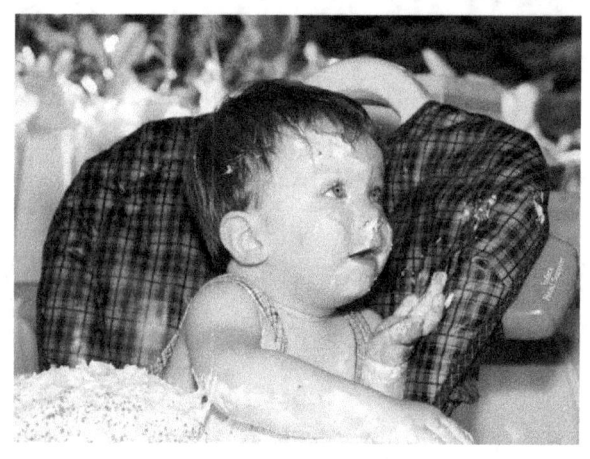

The Birthday Cake

By Essie Hudgins Jordan

Your birthday cake I could not bake.
The recipe on card please take.
It sounds so luscious and so rich,
I'm not so sure it is your dish.

In thought of calories one finds
the joy of eating left behind.
Life's bowl of cherries sweet or sour;
Take your pick; enjoy the hour.

Life's too short and time too fleet,
to be concerned with what we eat.
So fill your bowl up to the brim,
or keep your figure neat and trim!

A "Little Big" Mistake

By R. Olin Jackson

Since first my love I drew you near,
I've learned what makes my life so dear.
To some these words do not relate,
for some oft make a "slight" mistake.

When tossed upon the seas of life,
Men sometimes fail to do what's right.
They know the course their life should take,
but still they make a "slight" mistake.

In this world men sometimes stray,
They seek excitement for the day.
When her love they do forsake,
They make a "little big" mistake.

Life moves on; so swift the years.
From frittered youth oft spring sad tears.
Love her each day like it's your last,
And in the end you'll never ask,

What did my greed cause me to lose?
What errored options did I choose?
Did my desires and selfish traits,
Produce a "little big" mistake?

Men sometimes do contemplate,
a senseless course they'd like to take.
Lucky are the ones today
avoiding times of falling prey.

When we're old with hair of grey;
a day my dear is here you say.
Your love I'll guard what 'ere the cost;
Your love with me will not be lost.

The march of time can cause distress.
So many ways a sly temptress.
Love her each day like it's your last,
and in the end you'll never ask,

Why did her love I overlook?
Why is my life an empty book?
Did my desires and selfish traits,
cause me to make a "big" mistake?

The Barefoot Boy

By John Greenleaf Whittier

Blessings on thee, little man,
Barefoot boy, with cheek of tan!
With thy turned-up pantaloons,
And thy merry whistled tunes.

With thy red lip, redder still.
Kissed by strawberries on the hill,
with the sunshine on thy face,
through thy torn brim's jaunty grace.

From my heart I give thee joy, -
For I was once a barefoot boy!
Prince thou art, - the grown-up man
Only is Republican.

Let the million-dollared ride!
Barefoot, trudging at his side,
Thou hast more than he can buy
In the reach of ear and eye, -
Outward sunshine, inward joy:
Blessings on thee, barefoot boy!

Oh for boyhood's painless play,
Sleep that wakes in laughing day,
Health that mocks the doctor's rules,
Knowledge never learned of schools,

Of the wild bee's morning chase,
Of wild-flower's time and place,
Flight of fowl and habitude
Of the tenants of the wood;

How the tortoise bears his shell,
How the woodchuck digs his cell,
And the ground-mole sinks his well;
How the robin feeds her young,
How the oriole's nest is hung;

Where the whitest lilies blow,
Where the freshest berries grow,
Where the ground-nut trails its vine,
Where the wood-grape's clusters shine;

Of the black wasp's cunning way,
mason of his walls of clay.
And the architectural plans
Of gray hornet artisans!

For, eschewing books and tasks,
Nature answers all he asks;
Hand in hand with her he walks,
Face to face with her he talks,
Part and parcel of her joy, -
Blessings on the barefoot boy!

Oh for boyhood's time of June,
Crowding years in one brief moon,
When all things I heard or saw,
Me, their master, waited for.

I was rich in flowers and trees;
Humming-birds and honey-bees;
For my sport the squirrel played,
Plied the snouted mole his spade;

For my taste the blackberry cone
Purpled over hedge and stone;
Laughed the brook for my delight
Through the day and through the night,

Whispering at the garden wall,
Talked with me from fall to fall;
Mine the sand-rimmed pickerel pond,
Mine the walnut slopes beyond,
Mine, on bending orchard trees,
Apples of Hesperides!

Still as my horizon grew,
Larger grew my riches too;
All the world I saw or knew
seemed a complex Chinese toy,
Fashioned for a barefoot boy!

Oh for festal dainties spread,
Like my bowl of milk and bread;
Pewter spoon and bowl of wood,
On the door-stone, gray and rude!

O'er me like a regal tent,
Cloudy-ribbed, the sunset bent,
Purple-curtained, fringed with gold,
Looped in many a wind-swung fold;

While for music came the play
Of the pied frogs' orchestra;
And, to light the noisy choir,
Lit the fly his lamp of fire.
I was monarch: pomp and joy.
Waited on the barefoot boy!

Cheerily, then, my little man,
Live and laugh, as boyhood can!
Though the flinty slopes be hard,
Stubble-speared the new-mown yard,

Every morn shall lead thee through
Fresh baptisms of the dew;
Every evening from thy feet
Shall the cool wind kiss the heat.

All too soon these feet must hide
In the prison cells of pride,
Lose the freedom of the sod,
Like a colt's for work be shod,

Made to tread the mills of toil,
Up and down in ceaseless moil:
Happy if their track be found
Never on forbidden ground.

Happy if they sink not in
Quick and treacherous sands of sin.
Ah! that thou couldst know thy joy,
Ere it passes, barefoot boy!

Excerpt from *Gunga Din*

. . . . "And so I'll see him later on,
in the place where he has gone,
where it's always double-drill and no canteen.

"E'll be sittin' o'er the coals,
givin' drink to poor damned souls,
and I'd get a swig in Hell from Gunga Din.

"Yes it's 'Din,' 'Din,' 'Din,'
you Lazarusian leather Gunga Din.

"Though I've belted you an' flayed you,
by the eternal God that made you,
you're a better man than I am, Gunga Din."

– Rudyard Kipling, (1890)

Patton

"For over a thousand years Roman conquerors
returning from wars enjoyed the honor of triumph,
– a tumultuous parade. . . .

In one such instance, a slave stood behind the
conqueror, holding his golden crown
and whispering into his ear the warning,
that all glory is fleeting. . ."

– Gen. George S. Patton

Excerpt from *Intimations of Immortality from Recollections of Early Childhood*

. . . ."Then sing, ye birds, sing,
sing a joyous song!
And let the young Lambs bound
as to the tabor's sound!

"We in thought will join your throng,
Ye that pipe and ye that play,
Ye that through your hearts today
feel the gladness of the May!

"What though the radiance
which was once so bright
be now forever taken from my sight;

"Though nothing can bring back the hour
of splendour in the grass, of glory in the flower,
we will grieve not, but rather find
strength in what remains behind."

– William Wordsworth (1804)

"May the road rise up to meet you;
May the wind be always at your back;
May the sun shine warmly on your face;
And you sleep in the Lord's safe embrace."

– ancient Irish prayer

About The Author

R. Olin Jackson founded *Legacy Communications, Inc.*, in 1985, where he became the award-winning executive editor and publisher of his flagship creations – *North Georgia Journal* and *Georgia Backroads* magazines. He ultimately built these endeavors into the premier travel and history publications of Georgia.

During his tenure at *Legacy Communications*, Olin was the recipient of a number of awards from the *Magazine Association of Georgia (MAG)* for excellence in publishing. He parlayed this business endeavor into a long and fruitful career before selling it in 2005.

In 2021, Olin founded *Whippoorwill Publications, LLC*. His creations there include *Mystery & History in Georgia, Volume I* (2022) (honored with a *Five-Star Award by Readers' Favorite* book awards); *Mystery & History in Georgia, Volume II* (2023); *Some Genealogy Keys to Some Georgia Family Trees* (2023); *Memories of Army Life and MPs of the 529th* (2023); and *John Henry "Doc" Holliday* (2023). Other works in progress include *Gunmen, Lawmen and Wild Men of Early Georgia*.

Olin is married to the former Judy Grizzle of Dahlonega, Georgia. The couple make their home in Roswell, Georgia. Olin also has a son – Burke – by a former marriage.

All works by *Whippoorwill Publications* are available online at *Amazon.com, IngramSpark.com, BarnesandNoble.com*, and other fine booksellers.

Photos Index

(In Order of Appearance)

1. The Christmas cabin painting on the cover of *After All That We've Been Through* is the marvelous creative work of the very talented Tatiana Mack (YaneyaArt.com) of Alpharetta, Georgia. A family in a small rural farmhouse of northwest Georgia of the early 1950s is depicted. The children pictured are listening attentively on Christmas Eve as their father reads the enrapturing verse from *"A Visit from St. Nicholas,"* better known the world over as *"T'was the Night Before Christmas"* by Clement Clarke Moore.

2. The much-beloved family feline, "Prissy" (1996-2015), holds court at one of her favorite observation posts at 3617 Summit Oaks Drive in Roswell sometime around 2011. *"Through life's travails, its peaks and vales, our lives can seem so bleak. So few do pause in wondrous awe of all we take so cheap."* (Photo by Glenda Gail Dalton)

3. A late afternoon stroll down the lane at the old family farm. (Photo by Giuseppe Ramos)

4. The author's fishing cabin on Whippoorwill Hill in northwest Georgia, near the site of the farm upon which he was raised, is pictured. (Photo by the author)

5. A cardinal with its brilliant plumage scans the forest floor for a food opportunity in the dead of winter, 2016. *"So who created nature's theme?*

How do the creatures know? That's easy friend, so simple for, it's God that made it so!" (Photo by the author)

6. The Jackson family – (L-R): Mary, David, Olin, Guy and Patricia, photographed on the family farm in the spring of 1959. Guy would be gone from a drug overdose some 20 years later in 1980, and Mary in 2014 from the rare disease, MSA. Marilyn and Ralph died respectively in 2007 (from blood cancer) and 2011 (from natural causes). Patricia, David and Olin are now in their 70s. *"Spring-times of life seem so endless; when one is a child with no woes; but years slip away far too quickly, as children grow up and grow old."* (Photo by Marilyn Jackson)

7. The author spends a treasured moment with his little buddy and sidekick – grandson Alexander Jackson. Quick as a wink, they're grown and gone. (Photo by Judy Kay Jackson)

8. The marriage of R. Olin Jackson and Judy Kay Grizzle in Cumming, Georgia, on June 15, 1985. Thirty-nine years – and counting – as of 2024. Where have all the years gone, and how did they disappear so quickly? *"Yet each night when I do sleep; Each night in slumber oh so deep; Your love a treasure I do keep; Your love a treasure oh so sweet."*

9. James Larry Grizzle (1950-1997) watches over tiny sister Judy Kay Grizzle on a warm spring morning in 1956. *"Memories from springtime; Strawberries from the field; Laughter in our running; No worries yet revealed."* (Photo by Imogene Carder Cotton)

10. An ancient spear-point crafted a millennia ago by Native Americans, found near the author's fishing cabin on Whippoorwill Hill, Polk County, GA, in 2018. *"So heed my words; don't waste your time. Of this I strongly stress. Cause in the end you'll also find that Time's a harsh mistress."* (Photo by the author)

11. Grandpapa and grandchildren, Catherine and Alexander Jackson, can barely be contained for a moment to obtain yet another memory in a photograph. Little Sis has already spied a kitty in the distance she wants to pet. (Photo by Judy Kay Jackson)

12. Guy Wilfred Jordan and Essie Carroll Hudgins Jordan admire newborn Marilyn Jordan in the summer of 1928. This photograph was taken in the side-yard of the Jordan family residence at 215 Bluff Street, Rockmart, Georgia. In the distance to their rear, Rose Hill Cemetery in which they all three sleep today, is faintly visible. This historic residence, purchased by Guy and renovated in 1927, still exists in Rockmart as of this writing in 2024, and is at least 100 years in age. It was owned by Guy – and later by Essie – until 1999 when Essie passed away, one month shy of her 99th birthday. (Photographer unknown and long since departed)

13. Alexander Jackson pauses with Grandpapa during a celebration of his 6th birthday in Woodstock, Georgia. *"When we're at the end of life our 'stuff' we are forbidden. The only thing we 'keep' in Flight is the love we've given."* (Photo by Judy Kay Jackson)

14. Young Alexander Jackson was barely three years of age when his mother made this special cake for him at his birthday in Woodstock, Georgia. He just couldn't decide if it was more fun to put the cake and sweet icing in his belly, or on his face. *"Life's too short and time too fleet, to be concerned with what we eat."* (Photos by Olga Jackson)

15. The couple in this 1948 photo appear happy and carefree, but their selfishness, uncontrolled anger and overindulgences drove them to divorce in 1970 and rendered untold pain and suffering upon their children.

16. Little Caden Strahan sleeps blissfully, secure with "The Hulk." *"Oh for boyhood's painless play; sleep that wakes in laughing day; health that mocks the doctor's rules; knowledge never learned of schools."* (Photo by Nicole Strahan)

17. The dead trunks of tall sycamores are beautifully-reflected in the crystal clear waters of this pond in the wilds of northwest Georgia. *"The Lord giveth, and the Lord taketh away."* (Photo by the author)

18. Eight-year-old Olin Burke Jackson learned at his father's knee in 1985, how to catch and string fish on a cypress branch near his father's fishing cabin at Whippoorwill Hill in northwest Georgia. *"Blessings on thee, little man, barefoot boy, with cheek of tan! With thy turned-up pantaloons and thy merry whistled tunes."* (Photo by the author)

19. The author and an old Army buddy – First Sergeant Frank Withers – cool out after a hot day with family and friends at Whippoorwill Hill cab-

in and pond. *"Though I've belted you and flayed you, by the eternal God that made you, you're a better man than I am, Gunga Din."* (Photo by Mary Withers)

20. The author with fellow enlistees Sgt. Randy Roberts, Spec-4 Kyle Harris, Spec-4 Jack Williams, and Spec-4 Donald "Dutch" Wiersema of the U.S. Army's 529th Military Police Company, marching in formation in Germany, 1972. *". . . whispering into his ear the warning that all glory is fleeting."*

21. The author and wife, Judy, at the Old Lake Rabun Hotel in northeast Georgia. *"Though nothing can bring back the hour of splendour in the grass, of glory in the flower, we will grieve not, but rather find strength in what remains behind."* (Photo by Mary Withers)

22. The late Brig. Gen. Thomas Watson Dalton – a close friend of the author – takes one of his final walks with grandson, Pierce, at Anna Ruby Falls State Park in north Georgia in the autumn of 2006. *"May the sun shine warmly upon your face, and you sleep in the Lord's safe embrace."* (Photo by Glenda Gail Dalton)

Also by
R. Olin Jackson

and available from Amazon.com, BarnesandNoble.com, and IngramSpark.com and other fine booksellers

MYSTERY & HISTORY IN GEORGIA

VOLUME 2

R. OLIN JACKSON

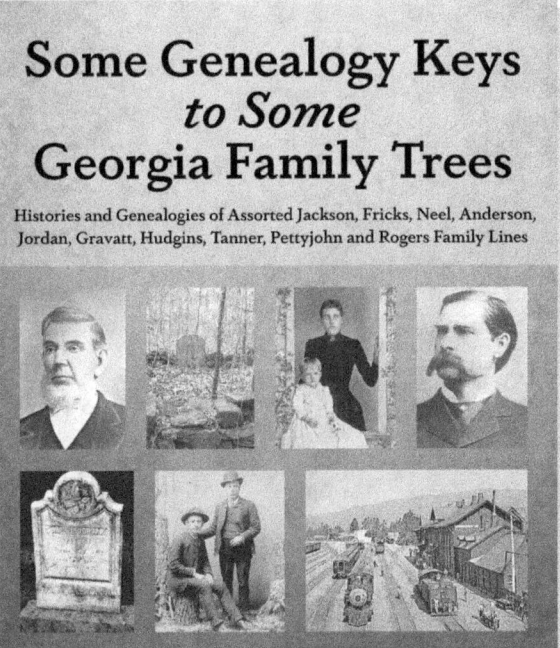

www.ingramcontent.com/pod-product-compliance
Lightning Source LLC
Chambersburg PA
CBHW070741060526
44119CB00070B/67